Write On!

WONDERFUL WORDS

Written by
Charis Mather

KidHaven
PUBLISHING

Published in 2026 by
KidHaven Publishing, an Imprint of
Greenhaven Publishing, LLC
2544 Clinton St., Buffalo, NY 14224

Written by: Charis Mather
Edited by: E.C. Andrews
Designed by: Jasmine Pointer

Cataloging-in-Publication Data
Names: Mather, Charis.
Title: Wonderful words/ Charis Mather.
Description: Bufalo, New York : Kidhaven Publishing, 2026. | Series: Write On! | Includes glossary and index
Identifiers: ISBN 9781534550483 (pbk) | ISBN 9781534550490 (library bound) | ISBN 9781534550506 (ebook)
Subjects: LCSH: Authorship—Juvenile Literature | Creative writing—Juvenile Literature | Vocabulary—Juvenile Literature
Classification: LCC PN159 M38 2026 | DDC 808.02-dc25

Manufactured in the United States of America

CPSIA compliance information: Batch #CSKH26
For further information contact Greenhaven Publishing LLC at 1-844-317-7404.

Please visit our website, www.greenhavenpublishing.com.
For a free color catalog of all our high-quality books, call toll free 1-844-317-7404 or fax 1-844-317-7405.

Find us on

Image Credits

All images are courtesy of Shutterstock.com, unless otherwise stated.

Cover – the8monkey, NotionPic, SpicyTruffel, TungCheung, The Paper Owl. Throughout – SpicyTruffel, NotionPic. 4–5 – Ground Picture, Kiselev Andrey Valerevich. 6–7 – Take Photo, OMD-project. 8–9 – Elena Sherengovskaya, pakww, Prostock-studio, Pixel-Shot. 10–11 – alexei_tm, A. Aleksandravicius, lemono. 12–13 – Ground Picture. 14–15 – Nuwat Phansuwan. 16–17 – Yuliya Evstratenko, Julia Savko. 18–19 – Krakenimages.com. 20–21 – TungCheung, Ground Picture. 22–23 – WESTOCK PRODUCTIONS, wavebreakmedia.

CONTENTS

Words that look like this can be found in the glossary on page 24.

A

C

YOU CAN WRITE

Hoot-hoot! Hello! I am Professor Hoot, a lover of language and a wiz with words. My job is to teach young learners like you how to write well.

You? Learn to write? That's right! Everyone can write if they want to. It just takes a bit of time to learn about language and the fascinating things it is made up of.

WHAT'S SO WONDERFUL ABOUT WORDS?

Have you ever read a story that lit up your imagination? Or heard a pun that made you grin from ear to ear? Or opened up a letter that told you something terrific?

Without words, none of that would be possible. Words allow you to express whatever you want however you want—just like painting! Writers have to pick their words carefully, just like artists picking colors.

WHY DO WORDS MATTER?

Different situations need slightly different words. For example, there are lots of different ways to say hello, but not every option works for every situation.

Feeling casual?

Feeling formal?

Feeling like a cowgirl?

Words have the power to change how people think, feel, and act. They can make people laugh or cry. The right words at the right time can make someone's day or turn it upside down.

HAVE YOU EVER GOT A MESSAGE THAT MADE YOU HAPPY?

KNOW YOUR NOUNS

Since words matter so much, you should know about some different kinds. Many sentences have nouns, so let's start there. I've marked some noun examples in orange.

Nouns are words that name things—such as girl, dog, ball, garden, and happiness.

Nouns name people, animals, things, and places. They can name things that are harder to picture, including feelings and ideas.

Nouns are usually found with words that give them more detail, called noun phrases.

ALL ABOUT ADJECTIVES

Some sentences are very plain. You can spice them up by adding words called adjectives. Adjectives describe nouns. They tell you about the look, smell, taste, sound, or feel of something, plus much more.

TRY NOT TO OVER-SPICE YOUR SENTENCES. JUST A FEW ADJECTIVES WILL DO!

Here are some adjectives I would use to describe Mrs. Hoot:

Look out for some examples of adjectives written in green.

wise

funny

charming

feathery

clever

gentle

kind

loving

patient

encouraging

helpful

shy

You can put adjectives before or after nouns.

VALUE YOUR VERBS

By now, you should be an expert at describing things in an exciting way. But how can you explain what happens to those things? That's where verbs come in. Verbs are action words.

EVERY SENTENCE NEEDS A VERB.

Some verbs tell you about actual actions. The more <u>specific</u> your action verbs are, the better your reader can picture them. Look at these examples of verbs in purple.

Swoop, hoot, chomp, and snooze are my favorite verbs.

Some verbs just tell you that something exists or how something is.

The baby owls are in the tree. It is warm in there.

ALL SORTS OF WORDS

Exclaim Your Emotions!

Exclamations are awesome! They are words that can be shouted out to get attention or to show strong feelings. Exclamation words are super useful when you are writing dialogue. I have written some examples of exclamations for you in blue.

Transition Words

Transition words are helpful when you are telling stories or giving instructions. Transition words link sentences or parts of sentences. They often explain what order events happen in. Look at these example transition words written in red.

Origami instructions use transition words such as the ones shown here!

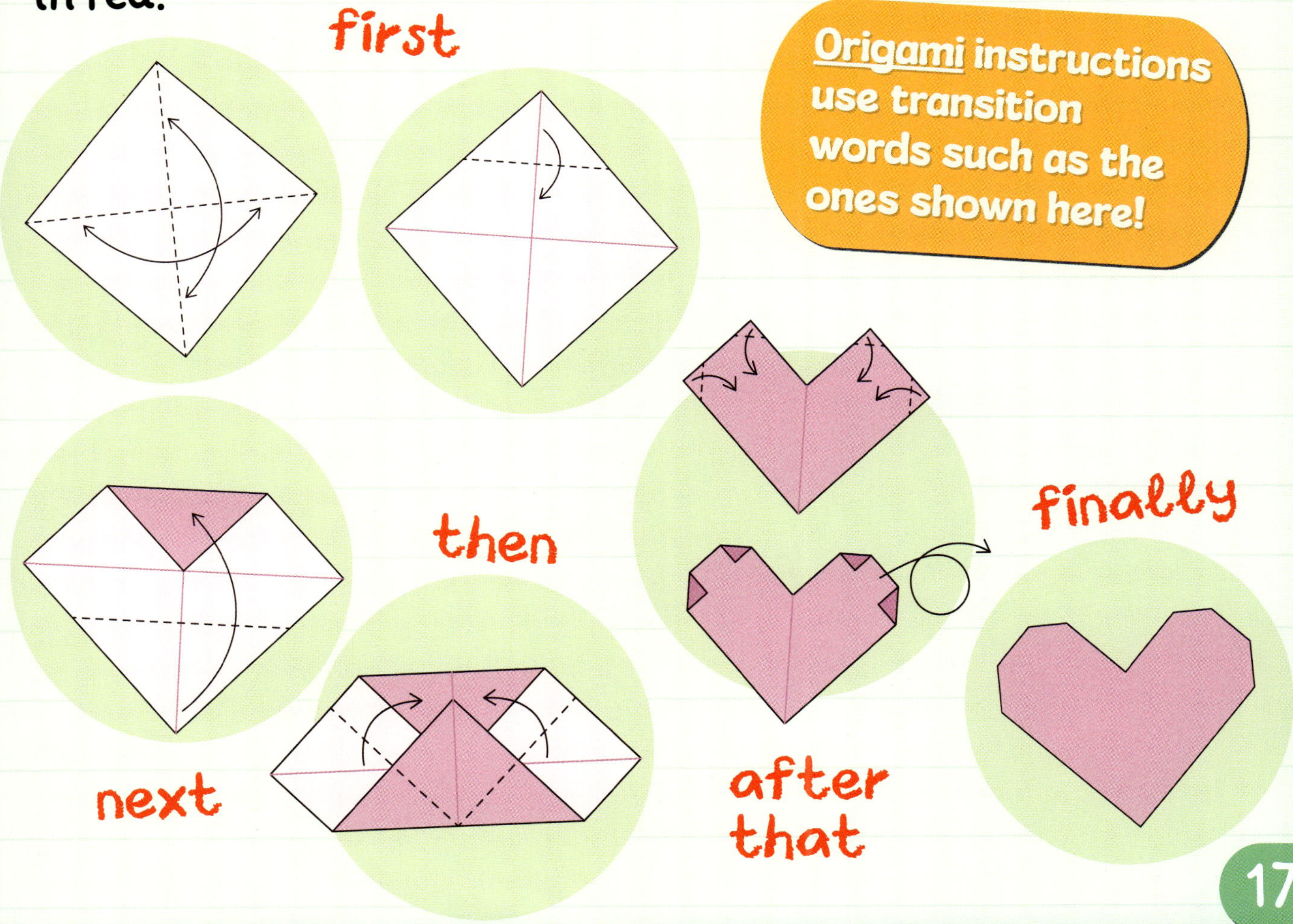

RHYME TIME

Have you ever tried writing your own song? Songs, riddles, and poems often use rhyming words. Rhyming words are words that sound the same at the end, such as sing and ring. I have put some example rhyming words in blue.

Here's a poem I wrote. Can you spot any rhyming words?

You may have heard of birds like **me**.
I am a bird called an owl, you **see**.
I sleep in the day and I teach at **night**.
It is my mission to help kids to **write**!

Hint: Check the end of each line.

PROFESSOR HOOT'S MOST HELPFUL TOOLS

When I write, I keep a few helpful tools close by. My dictionary is a book full of words and their meanings. Sometimes, I use it to learn new words to use in my stories.

DICTIONARIES CAN HELP YOU CHECK YOUR SPELLING TOO.

I also have a thesaurus. It helps me find words that have similar meanings to other words. I use my thesaurus to find more ~~exciting~~ sensational words to use. See what I did there?

WORDS THAT MEAN SIMILAR THINGS ARE CALLED SYNONYMS.

READ ON, WRITE ON

Aren't words just wonderful? With the right words, you can tell the world whatever you want. Not everyone thinks writing is easy, and that is OK. Keep practicing—it really is worth it.

PEOPLE LEARN AT DIFFERENT SPEEDS. FOCUS ON ONE WORD AT A TIME.

One of the best ways to learn new words is to read. Why not pick up some books and explore how different writers use words? It might <u>inspire</u> you. So read on, write on!

GLOSSARY

casual	relaxed, not fancy
dialogue	speech between characters
express	show or communicate thoughts or feelings
formal	to do with an important or serious event
inspire	make someone want to do something
origami	a type of art that involves folding paper in a set way to make different shapes
poems	pieces of writing that use creative language to share ideas and feelings; they can rhyme but do not have to
pun	a joke that depends on the different meanings of a word
riddles	questions or word puzzles that are difficult to figure out
specific	to do with a particular thing or way of doing something

INDEX